D0498397

TOO MANY BALLOONS

By Catherine Matthias

Illustrations by Gene Sharp

Prepared under the direction of Robert Hillerich, Ph.D.

CHILDREN'S PRESS
A Division of Grolier Publishing
Sherman Turnpike
Danbury, Connecticut 06816

Library of Congress Cataloging in Publication Data

Matthias, Catherine.
  Too many balloons.

  (A Rookie reader)
  Summary: A seven-year-old shares her color-
ful balloon collection, acquired one at a
time, with zoo residents.
  [1. Zoo animals—Fiction.   2. Counting.
3. Color.   4. Balloons-Fiction]   I. Sharp,
Gene, ill.   II. Title.   III. Series.
PZ7.M4347To   [E]   81-15520
ISBN 0-516-03633-5   AACR2

17 18 19 20 R 99 98 97

I went to the zoo.

I bought one red balloon.

I showed my one red
balloon to the lion.
He liked it.

I bought two yellow balloons.
I showed my two yellow
balloons to the giraffes.

They liked them.

I bought three blue balloons.
I showed my three blue
balloons to the seals.

They liked them.

I bought four green balloons.
I showed my four green
balloons to the crocodiles.

They liked them.

I bought five orange balloons.
I showed my five orange
balloons to the apes.

They liked them.

I bought six white balloons.
I showed my six white
balloons to the polar bears.

They liked them.

I bought seven pink balloons.
I showed my seven pink
balloons to the flamingos.

They liked them.

I bought eight purple balloons.
I showed my eight purple
balloons to the peacocks.

They liked them.

I bought nine striped balloons.
I showed my nine striped
balloons to the zebras.
They liked them.

I bought ten polka-dot balloons.
I showed my ten polka-dot
balloons to the pigeons.

I think I bought too many balloons.

WORD LIST

	lion	six
apes	many	sold
balloon(s)	my	striped
bears	nine	ten
blue	one	the
bought	orange	them
crocodiles	out	they
eight	peacocks	think
flamingos	pigeons	three
five	pink	to
four	polar	too
giraffes	polka-dot	two
green	purple	went
he	red	white
I	seals	yellow
it	seven	zebras
liked	showed	zoo

About the Author

Catherine Matthias grew up in a small town in southern New Jersey. As a child, she loved swimming, bicycling, snow, and small animals. *Wind in the Willows* and *The Little House* were her favorite books.

She started writing her own children's stories while teaching pre-school in Philadelphia. *Too Many Balloons* and *Out the Door* are her first published books.

Catherine now lives with her family in the Northwest, where her favorite things are gardening, hiking, fog, windy autumn days, and the ocean.

About the Artist

Gene Sharp has illustrated books, including school books, for a number of publishers. Among the books he has illustrated for Childrens Press are *The Super Snoops and the Missing Sleepers* and several in the "That's a Good Question" series.